WEST IND

BOOK ONE

BRER RABBIT MEETS THE TAR BABY.

(*See page 130.*)

NELSON'S

WEST INDIAN READERS

Book ONE

Compiled by J. O. Cutteridge

OXFORD
UNIVERSITY PRESS

PREFATORY NOTE FOR TEACHERS

IT is with considerable trepidation that I venture to place this little book—the first of a series of West Indian Readers—before teachers and pupils. The difficulty of the task of preparing such books as will make a common appeal to all the Caribbean, Guyana, and Belize is well known to all of you. I hope, nevertheless, that the series may help to supply a long-felt want—viz., that of local text-books specially prepared for West Indian schools. It has been my endeavour to include local names and terms whenever possible, as my experience has been that the pupils have great difficulty in spelling common words which they seldom, if ever, see in print. If alternative names are used in any colony they should be given by the teacher.

The series has several aims in view:—

(i) To provide matter with which the children are familiar in order that they may read the ideas expressed as well as the mere words.

(ii) To encourage reading with comprehension and develop initiative.

The exercises at the ends of the lessons should be treated as the most important part of the work. For the first few lessons direct guidance will be necessary from the teacher until the pupils grasp the idea. After that they should be encouraged to solve them unaided. The degree of success with which they are able to accomplish this will be a guide as to the intelligent grasp they have made of the subject-matter.

N.B.—It should be constantly borne in mind by teachers that committing the answers to memory will defeat the object in view. The value of the exercise lies in the *process* of obtaining the answer, not in the answer itself. Teachers should compile additional exercises on similar lines.

(iii) To serve as an introduction to literature and so encourage wider reading on the part of the pupil.

The books from which the extracts are taken should be obtained and used by the teacher to read to the children, and also for the more advanced pupils to read individually.

Those used in this book are:—

1. *Æsop's Fables.* Nelson's Reading Practice Series.

2. *Tales of Brer Rabbit.* Nelson's Reading Practice Series.

3. *Tales of Silly People.* Nelson's Reading Practice Series.

4. *Stories from Grimm.* Nelson's "Told to the Children" Series.

It will be noted that the orthodox lists of words and meanings are omitted. The meanings of words are best realized from the context, and difficulties in spelling differ in localities. Teachers should prepare their own lists from the lessons, and the pupils should see the words in the context rather than in isolation.

Lessons on plant and animal life have been treated in a general way to awaken the interest of the children in their surroundings. A more scientific treatment is left for nature-study lessons.

I acknowledge with deep gratitude the help I have received from inspectors of schools and teachers from various islands, Mr. L. O. Inniss of Trinidad for permission to utilize some of his Creole Folk-Tales, and all others who have assisted me in any way with matter and illustrations for the series. Without their help it would have been impossible to complete the task.

Suggestions for improvements or modifications for future editions will be gratefully received from teachers.

J. O. CUTTERIDGE

CONTENTS

An Asterisk (*) indicates Poetry

Acknowledgements

The author and the publisher would also like to thank the following for permission to reproduce material:

Images

p1: 'Mawnin' says Brer Rabbit (colour litho) Brer Rabbit (gouache on paper), Rountree, Harry (Herbert R.) (1878–1950)/Private Collection/The Bridgeman Art Library; p17: INTERFOTO/Alamy; p39: Tetra Images/Alamy; p48: Mary Evans Picture Library/ Grenville Collins Postcard Collection/Alamy; p50: Sean O'Neill/Alamy; p55: Ulrich Doering/Alamy; p56: M.D. Spooner; p60: Harry Rountree; p70: National Geographic Image Collection/Alamy; p73: Hulton Archive/Getty Images; p74: M.D. Spooner; p82: Robert Harding Picture Library Ltd/Alamy; p109: Harry Rountree; p128: The Princess and the Frog, 1894, Symonds, William Robert (1851–1934)/© Bradford Art Galleries and Museums, West Yorkshire, UK/The Bridgeman Art Library.

Every effort has been made to trace the copyright holders but if any have been inadvertently overlooked the publisher will be pleased to make the necessary arrangements at the first opportunity.

LESSON 1

TREES AND PLANTS

TREES and plants grow out of the ground. Their roots are in the ground. From their roots come the stems, and on the stems are the leaves, the flowers, and the fruit.

Here is a tree. We see leaves and fruit on it. We do not see its roots,

MANGO TREE

RICE

for they are in the ground. The tree is called a mango tree. The fruits on the tree are mangoes. Inside the mangoes are seeds, juice, and pulp.

Rice is a plant. It has stems, leaves, and seeds. It grows in water. The seeds of the rice plant are called rice. We eat rice; it is our food.

9

CORN

Corn is another plant. It also has a stem, leaves, and seeds, but it does not grow in water as rice does. It is sometimes called maize.

Another tree is the lime tree. Its fruit is called a lime. The juice of mangoes is sweet, but the juice of limes is sour, or acid, as some people call it. Girls and boys like mangoes and eat them, but they do not eat limes.

There are many seeds in a lime, but only one seed in a mango. The seed of a mango is called a stone; the seeds of a lime are called pips.

Men put seeds into holes in the ground, and plants or trees grow out of them. A mango tree grows from a mango stone, and a lime tree grows from a lime pip.

LIME FRUIT

Exercises

Fill in the blank spaces with the right words:—
1. I cannot see the ＿＿ of the tree.
2. I like the ＿＿ of the mango.
3. Some seeds are called ＿＿, and some are called ＿＿.
4. We eat ＿＿ and ＿＿ for our food. They are both seeds of plants.
5. The juice of some fruits is ＿＿, but that of others is ＿＿.
6. Both trees and plants have ＿＿, ＿＿, ＿＿, and ＿＿.

LESSON 2

FIRE AND WATER

FIRE is used in many ways. Without fire rice and plantains cannot be cooked, tea cannot be made, and bread cannot be baked. In cold countries fire is used to make people warm in winter.

Many useful things are made of iron and copper, and beautiful ornaments are made of gold and silver. These things are made by smiths, who all use fire.

Blacksmiths use it to make iron red-hot. The metal is then soft, and by hammering it they can make many things from it.

Railway trains are drawn by engines which are driven by steam. To make steam, water must be heated by fire.

We get fire by burning wood or charcoal. To make these burn we use matches. A match is a small piece of wood with a brown or red head, which catches fire and burns when it is rubbed.

Some matches are made in the West Indies, but most come from other countries, as the names on the boxes show.

We need water even more than fire. We need it for drinking, for cooking, for bathing, and for washing our clothes. Without water rice cannot be boiled, bread cannot be made, nor can we keep ourselves clean.

The farmers and planters also need it for their crops. Water falls on the earth as rain. In the southern West Indies most rain falls in the months from June to December. This is our rainy or wet season.

Much of the water which falls as rain runs into streams or creeks and rivers. Some of it is collected in tanks or vats. Some of it runs through the ground into wells or springs.

People bathe and wash their clothes in rivers, streams, and tanks, and use water from them and from wells for these purposes. In some towns and other places we get our water from pipes through taps. It comes from the water-works, where it is stored and from which it may be pumped.

EXERCISES

1. Make a list of the uses of fire, and another one showing the uses of water.
2. Enemies kill each other. Water kills fire, and fire destroys water. They are therefore ____.
3. How many months are there in the wet season? How many in the dry season?
4. If you had to do without fire or water, which would you choose to keep? Why?

LESSON 3

SEEDS

EVERY seed contains a young plant, which is safely covered up so as to protect it from harm. Some plants keep their babies in pods, like peas; some keep them in hard, rough shells, like coconuts; some in tough skins, like corn; and others in fruits, like the orange.

Some seeds grow in beautiful cups which split open to let out the seeds, or have little holes through which they fall out.

Others grow in pretty little boxes which have lids. When the seeds are ripe, the lids open with a snap. The wind shakes the box, and the seeds are scattered.

Look with care when you go out into the fields, or along the roads and paths, or through the woods or bush. You will see many pretty seed-boxes that Mother Nature has given to plants.

Plants of the same kind always have the same kind of pod, cup, or box; and we always find in them the same kind of seeds.

Fruits are really seed-boxes. On the outside they usually have a tough skin. What do you think this is for?

Inside a fruit you may sometimes find small flies, or even a bee or a wasp, eating the pulp. Something has made a little hole through the skin, and the insects have found this, and made it larger.

Most plants grow only from seeds, but some will grow from a stem or a root if it is put in the ground.

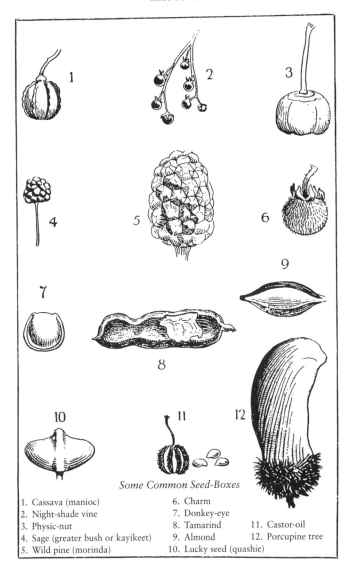

Some Common Seed-Boxes

1. Cassava (manioc)
2. Night-shade vine
3. Physic-nut
4. Sage (greater bush or kayikeet)
5. Wild pine (morinda)
6. Charm
7. Donkey-eye
8. Tamarind
9. Almond
10. Lucky seed (quashie)
11. Castor-oil
12. Porcupine tree

When a seed is placed in warm, moist ground the young plant grows and pushes its way out of the seed. It sends little roots down into the ground, and a tender shoot grows up into the air. A seed is really the egg of a plant.

In the seed itself there is a store of food on which the young plant can feed until its roots are strong enough to find food in the earth. Later on, leaves, flowers, and fruit grow on the plant.

On page 137 you will find a poem called "The Little Seed." You should read it after this lesson.

EXERCISES

I. Fill in the blank spaces:—
    1. ____ have their seeds in pods.
    2. ____ have their seeds in fruit.
    3. ____ have their seeds in tough skins.
    4. A seed will grow if it is kept ____ and ____, and covered with ____.
    5. Seeds contain ____ for the young plant.
II. Look at the pictures of seed-boxes on page 15.
    How many of these have you seen? Draw some of them. Collect some more seed-boxes.

LESSON 4

A PICTURE LESSON

Look at this picture. It shows a scene in the West Indies.

What *things* can you see in it?

How many *people* are there in the picture?

What is the boy doing? Do boys climb trees in this way in your country?

Look at the picture well and it will help you to put in the missing words in the rest of this lesson.

The boy is ___ some kind of tree. It is not a mango tree, a bread-fruit tree, a cocoa tree, a sugar-apple tree, nor a nutmeg tree, but it is a ___ tree.

The marks on the ___ prevent his feet from slipping, and he will soon be at the ___.

It is a very ___ tree, and has been bearing ___ for many years.

We cannot ___ many of the nuts as they are hidden by the leaves.

There are many ___ in the picture, but they are so close together that we cannot ___ them.

The ___ are all at the top of the tree. They look like a big ___ of feathers.

This picture was taken in Jamaica. Do you live in that country? If not, what country do you live in?

LESSON 5

WHAT A BIRD THOUGHT

I LIVED first in a little house,
  And lived there very well;
The world to me was small and round,
  And made of pale-blue shell.

I lived next in a little nest,
  Nor needed any other;
I thought the world was made of straw.
  And covered by my mother.

One day I fluttered from the nest,
   To see what I could find.
I said, "The world is made of leaves
   I have been very blind."

At last I flew beyond the trees,
   And saw the sky so blue;
Now, how the world is really made
   I cannot tell—can you?

Exercises

Write answers to the following questions:—

1. What was the bird's first house?
2. Where did it live next?
3. Why did it flutter from the nest?
4. What did it then think the world was made of?
5. Why did it think so?
6. What is the world really made of?

LESSON 6

THE CLOCK

HERE is a clock. Can you tell the time by it? If you cannot tell the time, you should now learn to do so.

First, you must learn the names of the figures on the dial or clock face. Here they are:—

I....1	IIII....4	VII....7	X....10
II....2	V....5	VIII....8	XI....11
III....3	VI....6	IX....9	XII....12

Now look again at the clock. It has two hands, a long hand and a short hand. The long one is called the minute hand, and the short one is called the hour hand.

A CLOCK

The long, or minute hand, goes from one figure to another in five minutes, and once round the clock in an hour. The short, or hour hand, takes a whole hour to go from one figure to the next.

If you look at a clock when it strikes the hour, you will see the minute, or long hand, pointing to XII; and the hour, or short hand, pointing to the number which the clock strikes.

To tell the time, you must look at both hands. The minute hand will tell you the number of minutes which have passed since the clock struck the hour. The hour hand will tell you the number of the hour which the clock struck last, and the number which it will strike next. You will see the hour hand between these two numbers.

From twelve o'clock at night till twelve o'clock the next night there are twenty-four hours. These twenty-four hours make a day. A day, then, is really a day and a night.

Twelve o'clock at night is the middle of the night; it is therefore called midnight. Twelve o'clock in the day is the middle of the day; it is therefore called midday, or noon.

Midday divides the day into two parts. We call the time before twelve morning and forenoon, and the time after twelve afternoon and evening.

Sixty minutes make an hour; twenty-four hours make a day; seven days make a week; and four weeks make a month.

Exercises

Read the lesson carefully to find the answers:—
1. What do these numbers mean on the clock— VI, IX, XI, and IIII?

2. How long does it take the short hand to go from I to III?
3. How long does it take the long hand to go from II to IX?
4. Which is the hour hand and which is the minute hand?
5. Where is the minute hand when the clock strikes?
6. How do you tell the time?

LESSON 7

MORE ABOUT TREES

HERE is a picture of a tree. The parts of a tree are its roots, trunk or stem, branches, and leaves. We find on some trees also flowers and fruit.

All trees have flowers at one time or other. Some have large, bright

A FOREST TREE

flowers, like those of the immortelle or cocoa shade tree; others have small flowers which are not easily seen, like those of the cedar.

We cannot see the roots of the tree, because they are hidden in the ground. They keep the tree upright, and fix it firmly in the ground, so as to prevent the wind from blowing it down.

The body of the tree without the branches is called the trunk. The branches grow out of the trunk. The very small branches are called twigs. From the twigs grow the leaves, the flowers, and the fruit.

The leaves of trees are very useful both to men and to animals. They give the shade that protects us from the heat of the sun; many animals feed on them; people cook food in the leaves of some trees, and they make mats from those of others.

The trunk and larger branches are also very useful. From them we get the wood, or timber, which is used in building houses and ships, and for making a large number of useful things. The smaller branches and twigs are used for firewood.

Many trees bear fruit which can be eaten; these are called fruit trees. We have mango trees, coconut trees, orange trees, bread-fruit trees, and tamarind trees, which bear mangoes, coconuts, oranges, bread-fruit, and tamarinds.

A great number of trees growing together is called a wood; a large wood is called a forest. In the West Indies we often call the forest the bush, or high wood; on the Main it is known as the jungle.

Proverb.— "As the twig's bent the tree's inclined."

Exercises

1. In the *Proverb,* "'s" means "is." Now write the proverb out in full.
2. Name all the parts of a tree which you have read of in this lesson.
3. Write one sentence about each of the following:—
   The use of the roots to the tree.
   The use of the twigs to the tree.
   The use of its leaves to men.
   The use of its trunk to men.
4. Write the names of all the fruit trees given in the lesson.
5. What is a forest?

LESSON 8

CREOLE FOLK-TALES—I

Introduction.—Folk-tales are stories which have been handed down from father to son by word of mouth for many years. Many of them have never been written. Such tales are found in all countries, but we do not know how they started. Perhaps they were made up to amuse the children. The folk-tales you will read in these Readers have been collected by Mr. L. O. Inniss of Trinidad from many old Creoles, and he has very kindly allowed me to tell them here for you.

How the Crab got that Crack in its Back

Once upon a time there were just two crabs in the world. One of them went down to the river one day to bathe, and there she saw a very old woman sitting on a log of wood.

"Scratch my back," said the old woman. Now she was not very pleasant to look at, and she did not say "please," but the crab was kind-hearted and did what the old lady asked.

This pleased her very much, and she then asked the crab to take a calabash and dip some water for her. The kind crab did so, and the old woman drank and was refreshed.

Now this old woman was a fairy. Perhaps you have guessed this already. She said to the crab, "You are a good, kind girl, and I will do

something for you now." So she sprinkled a few drops of water upon her, and the crab became a beautiful bird with gay feathers.

When she went home she told her sister what had happened, and the other crab then rushed down to the river to see if she could be changed into a bird also. There she saw the old woman sitting on the log.

"Scratch my back" said the old woman.

"No, indeed, I will not!" said the crab.

"Take a calabash and bring me some water," said the woman.

"Get it for yourself," said the rude crab.

This made the old woman angry, so she raised her stick and gave the crab such a whack on her back that it cracked the shell.

The marks of the crack remained on her children and are on all other crabs to this day. When you see them, remember that kindness and politeness pay best in the end.

Exercises

1. Was the old woman pretty? How do you know?
2. Who was pretty in the story?
3. Were these crabs male or female or one of each?
4. What do you think the other crab would say when she saw the bird?
5. What did the bird tell her?
6. What lesson do you learn from this little story?
7. Which way does the crack go in the crab's back— from side to side or front to back?

LESSON 9

INSECTS—I

I WONDER how many girls and boys know what an insect is. You could give me the names of some, I know, such as ants, flies, moths, butterflies, beetles, bees, wasps,[*] and mosquitoes. But do you know why all these are called insects?

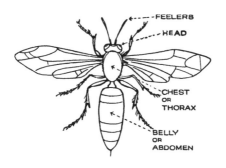

PARTS OF AN INSECT

It is easy to tell an insect by its legs alone, for it has always three pairs. So when you see a small animal with six legs you will know that it is an insect.

You can make quite sure by looking carefully at its body, which is always divided into three

---

[*] In British Guiana wasps are known as Marabuntas.

parts. The picture on page 29 shows these three parts very plainly. They are (1) the head, with its big eyes and two "feelers," (2) the chest or thorax, and (3) the belly or abdomen. Between these parts the body is very narrow.

Now examine any of the insects named in the first paragraph, and see if you can find these parts. Look at the picture, or at a real insect, and find out also to which of the three parts of the body the legs are joined. Sometimes you cannot see the legs very well, as they are behind the wings.

The legs are made up of a number of joints, and they often have little claws at the end.

Some insects have wings, but others have not. Can you give the names of any insects which do not fly?

Look at the head of the insect in the picture, and you will see a pair of large eyes. These large eyes are really made up of a number of very small eyes placed close together. Insects have a pair of small eyes also.

If you drop a piece of food on the floor, in a short time you will see hundreds of ants swarming round it. It is thus easy to believe that there are far more insects in the world than all the other animals put together.

They have many cousins which are very like them, but are not called insects. Some of these are spiders, worms, scorpions, crabs, and centipedes. Spiders and scorpions have eight legs and no feelers, and their bodies have only two parts. Crabs and others of their family have ten legs and four feelers. You know, too, that a centipede has many legs.

Exercises

1. Fill in the blanks by *one* word:—

> Insects have ____ eyes altogether.
> The legs are joined to the ____.
> If an insect loses two legs it has ____ left.

2. Do all insects have wings?
3. What do all insects have?
4. Which of these are insects—spider, ant, lobster, flea, and scorpion?

LESSON 10

THE NAUGHTY BOY

THERE was a naughty boy,
    And a naughty boy was he;
He ran away to Scotland
    The people there to see.

Then he found
That the ground
Was as hard
That a yard
Was as long,
That a song
Was as merry,
That a cherry

Was as red,
That lead
    Was as weighty.
That fourscore
    Was as eighty,
That a door
Was as wooden
As in England.

So he stood in his shoes
And he wondered,
He wondered;
He stood in his shoes
And he wondered.

JOHN KEATS

EXERCISES

1. Fill in the blanks:—

The ground is as ____ in ____ as in ____.
Lead is as ____ in the West Indies as in ____.
The door in the picture is ____.
Another name for eighty is ____.

2. What did the little boy expect to find when he reached Scotland?

3. Why did he stand and wonder and wonder?

LESSON 11

INDIA

MANY boys and girls who read this book are East Indians. Their parents or their grandparents came from India.

India is a country far away to the East, across thousands of miles of sea. It is divided between the two states of India and Pakistan. Ships come to us from India laden with rice for us to eat.

The people of India are brown in colour; some are very dark, others are almost white.

The country is very large, and millions of people live in it. Most of them live in villages and have small farms. On these farms they grow rice, corn, wheat, and other grains, and vegetables of various kinds.

Some of the people live in big cities, where there are fine temples and other beautiful buildings. Those who are rich live in fine houses. They wear dresses of silk, and jewels made of gold, silver, and precious stones. They ride on elephants.

The poor people live in houses built of mud and roofed with straw. They ride in carts drawn by bullocks.

In summer the days are very hot and people do not wear many clothes. They bathe themselves and sit in cool, shady places.

In winter the nights are very cold. The people then have fires to keep warm, and cover themselves with thick blankets when they go to bed.

A Hindu boy wears a turban, a shirt and a "dhoti," while his pretty sister wears an "orhni" or a beautiful "sari." The girl standing in the picture has an orhni on her head and shoulders, and the one sitting has a sari covering her head and body.

In India most boys do not choose the kind of work they would like to do, but they follow their father's trade. If a boy's father is a merchant, he also will become a merchant; but many of them study hard and become learned men.

The dishes and cups which the people use are made of bronze or of brass.

The water which they use in their houses is drawn from deep wells, and kept in earthen jars.

The people of India eat the food which they grow in their own country. They cook the vegetables in either mustard-oil, cottonseed oil, or ghee and massala.

The bigger children and grown-up people use a great deal of "dahi," which is prepared from the milk of the cow, while the younger children drink fresh milk every morning and evening.

Note.—A *dhoti* is the garment covering from the waist to the knee or ankle. A *sari* is the chief garment of a Hindu woman. An *orhni* is a kind of veil covering the head and arms. *Dahi* is curds or sour milk.

Exercises

1. What is the colour of the orhni worn by the girl in the picture?
2. What things can you see in the picture which you read of in the lesson?
3. What things can you see which were not mentioned?
4. Fill in the blanks:—

    The man nearest to you in the picture has a ____ turban.

    There is one animal in the picture. It is an ____.

    Behind the houses are some ____.

    The girl has ____ on her arms and ____ in her ears. Her skirt is ____.

A STREET IN INDIA.

LESSON 12

THE BAMBOO

IF anyone told you that the pages of this book were once *growing* in the West Indies you would find it hard to believe him. It is quite possible, however, that it would be true, for the printers had a very large plantation of bamboos in Trinidad, and from these bamboos paper was made.

You may also be surprised to learn that the bamboo belongs to the grass family, for we think of grasses as being small plants. This, however, is also true, and we might go on to say that the bamboo is a cousin of the Guinea grass, corn, rice, and sugar-cane, for they are all grasses.

All brothers and sisters are not exactly alike, and yet they are like each other in some way. So are all these grasses. All their roots are bunches of thin fibres like threads, while the stems of all are jointed and most of them are hollow. The sugar-cane, maize, and a few others have solid stems. Their leaves are long, narrow, and pointed, and have no stalks, but are wrapped round the stem.

BAMBOOS IN JAMAICA
(Inset—*Stem and Section*)

Look at any of these plants which I have called grasses, and see how and where the leaves grow.

The bamboo has underground stems also and from these many leaf-shoots spring up to form upright stems. You can thus see how it is that the bamboo grows in clumps. You may have seen many of them, as they can often be found near streams. When their heads meet they form graceful archways over the cool water beneath.

It is not only for making paper that this plant is useful, but for many other things.

What do you use as a flower-pot for young seedlings? Why, a piece of bamboo sawn across just below the joint.

What do we use for making fences, sheds, small bridges, ladders, masts for boats, and even houses? Why, again it is our useful friend the bamboo—the giant grass.

Exercises

1. Name some members of the "grass family."
2. Make a little drawing to show what is happening *under* the ground near a clump of bamboos.
3. What are bamboos used for?
4. Give the word which means the opposite to "giant."
5. In what ways are all grasses alike?
6. Make a drawing to show where you cut a bamboo to form a flower-pot.

AGOUTI

LESSON 13

CREOLE FOLK-TALES—II

How the Agouti* lost his Tail

ONCE upon a time all the horned animals decided to take a trip by sea. Only those with horns were invited, as they were thought to be the best of the beasts.

Now the dog and the agouti were close friends, and shared the same rooms like brothers. Of course they were not invited to the grand voyage to the island, for they had no horns. They were sulky at being left behind, especially Mr. Dog. He

---

* In some islands the agouti is known as "the Indian rabbit."

brooded over it, and at last thought of a plan to join the trip.

His plan was to make horns from cardboard and stick them on to his head. His friend Mr. Agouti helped him, and all went well as Doggie boldly walked on board, being taken for a kind of Saanan goat.

Seeing how easily his friend had succeeded, Mr. Agouti, like a mean fellow, became jealous, and as the boat pushed off he shouted, "There's a traitor on board! Examine the horns!"

At first no-one took any notice of him, but as he kept on shouting, Captain Bull ordered all the passengers to show their horns. Then the false horns of Mr. Dog were discovered, and they decided he should be put off the boat at once.

So Captain Bull, with a skilful butt, tossed him overboard. (Perhaps that is the reason why a dog always barks at a bull and tries to bite his nose.) Poor old Mr. Dog had then to swim hard for the shore.

He vowed he would have revenge on his friend for the trick he had played, but Mr. Agouti did not wait for his landing, as he knew what sharp teeth Mr. Dog had. So he wisely took the road

inland, followed hard by the dog, who meant to
pay him back.

The chase went on for a long distance until
the evening of the second day. The agouti had

almost reached the forest, and was just diving
into his burrow, when the dog made a sprint,
grabbed his long tail before it disappeared, and
bit it off short.

You see it has remained like that even to the
present day, and since then the dog and the
agouti have been sworn enemies.

"Never betray your friend."

Exercises

1. What animals do you think would be in the party?
2. How would the captain know the dog's horns were false?
3. Why did the agouti make off for his hole?
4. Why did the dog bite off the tail of the agouti?
5. Fill in the blanks:—

    The captain of the ship was a ___.

    He can ___ with his horns.

    The agouti's home was in the ___.

    The ___ and the ___ do not love each other.

    The dog saved its life by ___.

LESSON 14

THE MONGOOSE

Many years ago there were no mongooses in the West Indies. Their home is India. They live on snakes there, and in a book of Indian tales* you may read some day a very good story of a pet mongoose named "Rikki-tikki-tavi," who saved the life of a little boy.

They were brought here to kill off the rats, which did so much harm to the sugar-canes.

---

* *The Jungle Book,* by Rudyard Kipling

This they did very easily, but in another way they came to be a great trouble to us.

When rats became scarce the mongoose took for its prey lizards and birds, many of which feed on insects and ticks, and on grass-lice, which are young ticks. We now suffer from swarms of ticks,

MONGOOSE

grass-lice, and various insects, which before were eaten by birds and lizards.

The mongoose is often found about houses, and lives in holes dug by itself. It also makes its home in thickets near cocoa trees, and in the tall grass and bush of old sugar-cane fields.

Its food consists of lizards, rats, crabs, eggs, and the young of birds, such as the ground-dove, which make their nests on the ground. In the dry season, when insects, crabs, and frogs are scarce, it attacks poultry, and even eats fruit and vegetables.

The mongoose only hunts by day, and the artful rat, which has now learned to hunt by night, is safe from it.

In St. Lucia the fer-de-lance snake was a great danger until the coming of the mongoose. When the first two arrived many people thought such tiny creatures would be no match for this dangerous snake. So they were tried with one before being set free in the forests.

A cage containing the two mongooses, and a glass jar in which was a big fer-de-lance three feet long, were opened together. One mongoose at once bolted and was never seen again, but the other faced the reptile bravely. A great battle followed, but the mongoose proved the winner, and swallowed some inches of his enemy head foremost.

Exercises

1. Fill in the blanks:—

     The mongoose was brought to the West Indies to kill ____ and ____.

     It catches its food during the ____.

     The mongoose is an ____, but the snake is a ____.

2. Have you seen a mongoose? If so, what can you say about its colour, its size, and its tail?

3. A bird whose nest was in the branches of a tree found that its eggs had been sucked. Do you think a mongoose had done this? Why?

4. Why does the tree-rat hunt by night?

5. What beings were glad when the mongoose came?

LESSON 15

ANOTHER PICTURE LESSON

Look with care at everything you can see in the picture on the next page. Fill in the right words in the blank spaces below. Only one word is to go in each space.

    There are three animals and five —— in the picture.

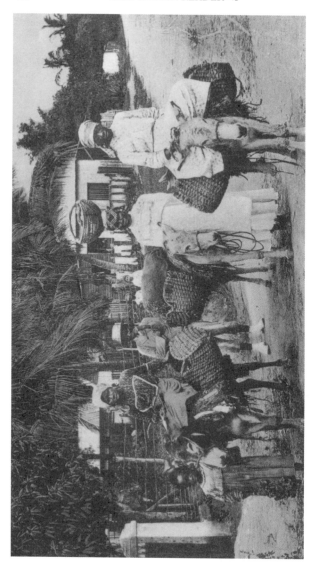

The animals are ___, but one of the
___ is ___ and the other two are ___.

Two donkeys have people on their ___,
but all donkeys have ___ on their backs.

One lady has a ___ on her head.

The people are in the sun, so most of them
have ___ their heads.

Two of the animals are facing forwards but
the other one is facing towards the ___. All the
people are facing ___.

Perhaps there are some ___ in the panniers on
the donkeys' backs.

What things can you see in the picture that
have not come in the lesson? Write the names of
them all.

Can you give a good title for this picture?

COCONUT TREES ON THE SEA-SHORE

LESSON 16

THE COCONUT TREE

WHERE do we find that the coconut palm grows most? Why, near the sea-shore or other damp places. People say that it likes to have its roots in water, and, best of all, in salt water.

The stem is long, and is often curved. Near the shore it seems to lean towards the sea, as if to meet the force of the wind and enjoy the breeze.

The leaves are all found at the top, and they look like a bunch of large feathers. When they fall off they leave rings on the stem of the tree.

Where do the flowers grow on this tree? What colour are they? If you do not know, you must look carefully at some trees to find the answers.

You have all seen the nuts growing on the tree, and know what they are like. They are covered with a hard, smooth rind, which is green at first, but becomes brown as the nuts ripen. Inside the rind there is a thick layer, which is white and tough when the nut is young, but which becomes dry and fibrous when the nuts are ripe. Inside this fibrous covering is the true nut or seed of the tree.

The thick covering or husk of the nut is stripped off, and beaten to separate the fibres. These are then used for making mattresses, or they are twisted or spun into rope or coarse twine, which is made into mats. This fibre is called coir. In the West Indies not much use is made of coir, and this part is mostly thrown away.

The seed or nut is contained in a hard shell. At one end of the shell there are three eyes. One is

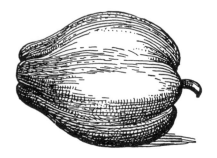

COCONUT IN HUSK   CROSS SECTION OF NUT

soft, and can be opened with a knife. You know that every seed contains a young plant, and the young coconut plant lies underneath this soft eye of the nut. When the coconut is put into a warm, damp place for a few weeks the young plant begins to grow. It sends out through the soft eye its young roots and a sharp-pointed shoot, and these pierce their way through the husk.

The roots grow down into the soil, while the shoot throws out green leaves. The roots get water and food from the soil to nourish the young plant, but for a long time the plant remains attached to the nut by means of a sucker which fills up the whole of the hollow space inside the nut. This sucker slowly takes up all the food which is contained in the white kernel of the nut, and passes it on to the young plant, which thus gets food from the nut as well as the water and other things which it gets from the ground by means of its roots.

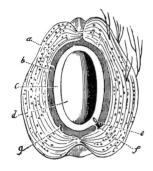

COCONUT,
VERTICAL SECTION

a, husk; *b*, shell; *c*, kernel, or white meat; *d*, hollow containing "milk"; *e*, young plant; *f*, the soft eye; *g*, one of the other eyes.

When the nuts are ripe they are gathered and broken open for the sake of the white meat, or kernel, which they contain. This is taken out and dried, either in the sun or in driers heated by fire. The dried meat is known as copra. Oil is got from it, which is used for cooking food by frying; it can also be used for making soap or candles; and much of it is used for making margarine, which can take the place of butter.

Before the nuts are ripe they contain a good deal of water, or, as it is sometimes called, milk. This is a very refreshing drink, and when the unripe coconuts are cut for obtaining this, they are called water-nuts.

The empty shells of the nuts are often cleaned, and used as drinking cups. Sometimes they are carved and polished, and look very pretty.

The dry leaves of the coconut are very useful for making mats or for covering roofs. The trunks are often cut up into boards. It is said that every part of the coconut palm is useful, so it is often called the "Prince of Palms," and it well deserves this name.

EXERCISES

I. Fill in the blanks:—
    1. The coconut is the "____ of Palms."
    2. Under the soft eye is the ____ ____.
    3. The flesh is called the ____.
    4. There are ____ questions in this lesson.

5. The milk is really ____ for the ____ plant.
6. The coconut is the —— of the tree.
7. The tree bends —— the sea.

II. (*a*) Count the nuts on a good tree. Most trees give about 80 to 100 nuts in a year.

(*b*) Ask your teacher to grow a young plant from a coconut. Note how the roots and the shoot come out. See if the young plant grows as this lesson tells you.

(*c*) Why has the nut both a husk and a shell?

GRADING COCONUTS

I found my poor little doll dears
As I played on the heath one day.

LESSON 17

THE LOST DOLL

I ONCE had a sweet little doll, dears,
   The prettiest doll in the world;
Her cheeks were so red and so white, dears,
   And her hair was so charmingly curled!
But I lost my poor little doll, dears,
   As I played in the heath one day;
And I cried for her more than a week, dears,
   But I never could find where she lay.

I found my poor little doll, dears,
   As I played in the heath one day;
Folks say she is terribly changed, dears,
   For her paint is all washed away,
And her arm trodden off by the cows, dears
   And her hair not the least bit curled;
Yet for old sake's sake she is still, dears,
   The prettiest doll in the world.

CHARLES KINGSLEY

EXERCISES

1. Who is speaking these lines? Who are the "dears"?
2. Had the little girl seen *all* the other dolls in the world?

3. Where was the little girl playing? What was there on the ground round about her as she played?
4. Had she any playmates?
5. Do you think it would be easy to find where the doll lay? Why?
6. What took the curl out of the lost doll's hair?
7. Which lines come twice over in these verses?
8. What are the sheep and cow doing in the picture?
9. Why is the cow only as broad as the girl's face?
10. Which is nearer to the girl, the first sheep or the cow?
11. Are the sheep all at the same distance from the girl?
12. Have you anything that you love "for old sake's sake"?
13. Has the girl in the picture just found the doll, or is she playing with it before it was lost? How do you know?
14. Describe the little picture below.

LESSON 18

A TALE OF BRER RABBIT

Introduction.—Here is a good story of Brer Rabbit and Brer Fox. The fox is a very sly animal, but he found that the rabbit could be artful too. They had many a battle, and you can read about their tussles in a fine little book called *Tales of Brer Rabbit.* Two more of the stories are given in the reading tests at the end of this book, on pages 130 and 132.

Brer Rabbit in the Well

One day when Brer Rabbit and Brer Fox, and Brer Coon and Brer Bear, and a great many others, were clearing some ground to plant seeds in, the sun began to get hot, and Brer Rabbit became tired; but he didn't tell the others, because he was afraid they would call him lazy. So he kept on pulling weeds and piling them up, until by-and-by he called out that he had got a thorn in his hand. Then he slipped away to find a cool place in which to rest.

The others thought he had gone to bathe his hand, and went on working. Brer Rabbit chuckled to himself, and ran on. After a while he came to a well with a bucket hanging in it.

"That looks cool in there," said Brer Rabbit, "and cool I expect it is! I think I'll just jump into

that bucket and have a sleep." And with that he jumped in. But no sooner was he in the bucket, than it began to go down the well!

It went down and down, and half-way down Brer Rabbit saw another bucket coming up, for the well was worked by a sort of see-saw arrangement of buckets. As one went down, the other came up. Well, Brer Rabbit's bucket went on down, and he began to be afraid he would drown when he reached the water. But when the bucket hit the water, it floated on the top, and there it stayed. Brer Rabbit kept very still, because he thought the bucket might fill with water if he moved! He just lay there quiet, but he couldn't help shaking and shivering.

Now Brer Fox always kept his eye on Brer Rabbit, and when he saw him slip off, Brer Fox thought he'd go after him and see where he was going. So he crept off and watched him. He saw Brer Rabbit come to the well and stop, and then he saw him jump into the bucket, and then, lo and behold! he saw him go down out of sight! Brer Fox was the most astonished fox in the world! He sat back in the bushes and thought and thought, but he *couldn't* make out why Brer Rabbit had gone down there like that.

Then he said to himself—

"Well, never did I see such a queer thing! I do believe Brer Rabbit keeps his money hid in that well; and if it isn't that, well, he must have discovered a gold-mine; and if it isn't that, then I'm going to see what it is!"

So Brer Fox crept a little nearer and listened, but he heard nothing; and he crept nearer and nearer still, and yet he heard no sound. By-and-by he crept right up to the well and peeped down, but he could see nothing and hear nothing.

All this time Brer Rabbit was scared nearly out of his skin, and he dared not move, in case the bucket should be upset and throw him in the water. Then suddenly he heard old Brer Fox call out—

"Hey ho! Brer Rabbit! Whom are you calling on down there?"

"Who? Me? Oh, I'm just fishing," said Brer Rabbit. "I said to myself that I'd give you all a surprise by getting you fish for dinner, so here I am, and here are the fishes! I'm fishing for sprats!"

"Are there many of them down there?" asked Brer Fox.

"Lots of them, Brer Fox, lots of them. The water is all alive with them. Come down and help me to catch them, Brer Fox," said Brer Rabbit.

"But how can I get down, Brer Rabbit?"

"Oh, jump into the bucket, Brer Fox, and it will bring you down all safe and sound!"

Now Brer Rabbit talked so happily and sounded so jolly, that Brer Fox jumped into the bucket, and, of course, down it went, and because he was heavier than Brer Rabbit his weight pulled Brer Rabbit's bucket up! When they passed one another half-way, Brer Rabbit sang out—

"Some go up and some go down, Brer Fox! You'll get the fishes all right!"

When Brer Rabbit got out, he ran off and told the folks who owned the well that Brer Fox was down their well making their drinking water all muddy. Then he ran to the well and called out to Brer Fox—

"Here comes a man with a great big gun!
When he pulls you up, you jump and run!"

And that's just what Brer Fox did, and in about half an hour both of them were back at work, weeding and planting, as if they had never heard of wells or buckets in their life; but every now and then Brer Rabbit would burst out in a laugh and look slyly at old Brer Fox!

Exercises

1. Why did—
   - (*a*) Brer Rabbit slip away from the work?
   - (*b*) Brer Fox creep after him?
   - (*c*) Brer Fox go down the well?
   - (*d*) Brer Rabbit run back to the well?
2. Can you see Brer Fox in the picture? What is he doing?
3. Try to make a little model of the well-head that will work.
4. This story shows the fox as greedy and foolish. How is each shown?
5. Write the line from the story that would just fit the picture on page 60.
6. Write the words that would fit the picture below.

LESSON 19

SOME OF OUR ANIMAL FRIENDS

WHAT should we do without our animal friends? The cow and the goat give us milk, and we eat their flesh when they are killed. Their skins are dried and sent away to be made into leather for boots and shoes, or harness for horses and donkeys. Perhaps you have seen bales of hides, as the dry skins are called, being loaded on to big steamers, or sloops.

Many boys and girls have to tie up their goats before going to school in the morning, and help to milk them in the afternoon.

You have all seen the Zebu bulls or oxen drawing carts.

The sheep is very like the goat, but its flesh, which is called mutton, is more tender to eat. The wool from its back is woven into cloth.

What a useful animal the donkey or ass is! It is a common sight to see boys or even men riding on this animal as it jogs along the country roads. Do you notice how they sit on the hind part of its back? Why is this?

In the cocoa-fields and on the estates we see the donkey with a crook and panniers on his back doing his share of the work in crop-time.

He has a bigger relative, the mule, which is somewhat like both an ass and a horse. Look at one carefully and find out in what ways it is like these animals. The mule is very stubborn, but is easily trained to be useful.

Animals which carry loads on their backs are called beasts of burden. The horse is one of the best of them. It can also draw heavy loads for us. Like all the other animals we have named, it feeds on plants such as grasses. Its teeth are made for this purpose. The hoof of the horse is not split or cloven like the hoofs of goats, cows, and sheep, but it is solid.

Among our pets are the cat and the dog. The cat has nice smooth fur, and it purrs when we stroke it. It has sharp teeth and claws to seize and tear its prey, for it lives on birds and small animals such as mice or rats. Little kittens are very playful creatures.

1 SHEEP   2 CAT   3 GOAT   4 DOG   5 ZEBU   6 COW
7 DONKEY   8 HORSE   9 MULE

The cat has some big wild cousins on the Main, where they roam about in the forests. They are the puma, the jaguar, the ocelot, and the tiger-cat. In other countries there are lions, tigers, panthers, and leopards, which are all very like our little friend the cat. They belong to the cat family.

Perhaps our best animal friend is the dog. He is very faithful, and guards our homes and gardens well. He follows the steps of his master or mistress, and trots along beside the pony when his master is riding. Like the cat he is a flesh-eater.

In Book Two you will read of some of our wild animals. All those named in this lesson are called domestic animals, except the wild cousins of the cat.

Exercises

1. How many animals are named in this lesson? Write out the names of them all.
2. Why is the lion said to belong to the cat family?
3. Fill in the missing words in the blank spaces:—

    The cow has a ____ hoof.

    The dried ____ of animals are called hides.

    That man is as ____ as a mule.

    The ____ belongs to the same family as the ass and the horse.

    ____ and ____ are wild cousins of the cat.

    Animals have the right kind of ____ for the food they eat.

LESSON 20

AMONG THE COCOA

WHAT is that sound which wakens us? Some one is blowing a conch-shell to call the workers to the cocoa-fields. It is only six o'clock, and the mist still clings in the valleys.

The sun will not be over the hills for another hour, so let us join the labourers in the cool air and go by way of the mule-track to the higher land in the middle of the estate.

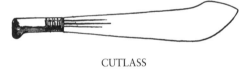

CUTLASS

GOULET   It is crop-time, and the men carry long cocoa-knives or goulets, which look like hands of steel on bamboo poles. Both men and women have a cutlass each; in Belize it is known as a *machete*.

Now they are hard at work gathering the pretty pods, some of which are red, while others are yellow, green, or purple. Those high up on the trees are cut off by the goulets and the lower ones by cutlasses.

See how careful the men are not to damage the eye on the tree where the pod grows. If this is cut it will not bear a pod there again.

BREAKING THE COCOA

In a nice cool spot near a stream the women are busy "breaking the cocoa," or opening the pods. How clever and quick they are at doing this and taking out the beans!

Here is a good pod we can look at. See how the beans inside it are neatly fitted together in five rows. The ridges on the outside of the pod are ten in number, two ridges to each row of beans. When we have time we will look at some more pods and see if they are all like this. The beans are pink in colour, and if we taste one we shall find it somewhat bitter.

FLOWER, POD AND SECTIONS

Now let us count the beans. There are just forty in this pod. The planter says they do not always have exactly this number, although very near it.

What are those donkeys doing with crooks and panniers on their backs? They are taking the beans down to the cocoa-house, where they will be placed in the sweat-boxes for a few days.

Let us go there and see some beans which have been sweated. We find they are no longer pink, but brown, and have lost their bitter taste.

Look at the large trays or drying-floors, where the beans are laid out to dry in the sun. Why are those men pushing the covers over the trays so quickly? Ah! rain is coming, and the beans must not get wet.

Inside the shed we can see other men busy putting the dried beans into bags ready to send away in ships to other countries. There they will be made into cocoa and chocolate. In another lesson, perhaps, we shall read how this is done.

If we go to the fields after the crop is over we shall see the men "cutlassing" or cleaning the land and the trees.

Look at the little pinky-white flowers on the stem of the tree. They seem too small ever to grow into cocoa-pods, but they will do so. Count the little petals and you will see that there are five.

The planter tells us the real name of the tree is *cacao*. He says that those big trees overhead are to give shade to the cacao beneath. In Grenada, where most of the trees are on hilly slopes, they have no shade trees, but the cacao is planted closer together than in the other islands.

Exercises

1. Draw a cutlass and a goulet.
2. Take three good pods, break them and count the beans in each. Add the numbers all together and divide by three.
3. Fill in the blanks:—

> Where the pod grows from the tree is called the ____.
>
> The beans are ____ five rows.
>
> Boucan is another name for the trays or ____.
>
> In ____ there are no shade trees for cocoa.
>
> The tree from which we get cocoa is called the ____.

REAPING COCOA

"ALL MY TOYS BESIDE ME LAY."

LESSON 21

THE LAND OF COUNTERPANE

WHEN I was sick and lay a-bed,
I had two pillows at my head,
And all my toys beside me lay,
To keep me happy all the day.

And sometimes for an hour or so
I watched my leaden soldiers go,
With different uniforms and drills,
Among the bed-clothes, through the hills.

And sometimes sent my ships in fleets
All up and down among the sheets;
Or brought my trees and houses out,
And planted cities all about.

I was the giant great and still
That sits upon the pillow-hill,
And sees before him, dale and plain,
The pleasant land of counterpane.

From "A Child's Garden of Verses," by
ROBERT LOUIS STEVENSON

Exercises

1. Name each of the toys. How many soldiers are shown? How many different uniforms? What is meant by "through the hills"?
2. Is there a "fleet" of ships in this picture?
3. What does the boy mean by "sometimes sent my ships in fleets"?
4. What toys would he need to make up a city?
5. Why does he call himself a giant?
6. What is meant by a "dale" and a "plain"?
7. How many lines are there in this poem? How many verses? How many lines to each verse?
8. Which of the lines do you like best?
9. What do you notice about the sounds at the ends of the lines?
10. Can you think of a word with the same sound as pane; pills; post; house; hard; eye?
11. What do you notice about the first letter in each line?
12. Make a drawing of a toy soldier standing on guard.
13. Try to write a verse to add to this poem. Perhaps you might begin:—

 When daylight goes, nurse draws the blind.
14. Or you might write a verse, or perhaps two verses, of your own about this picture.

LESSON 22

ÆSOP'S FABLES—I

About Æsop and his Stories

More than two thousand years ago there was born in Greece a little boy slave called Æsop. This little slave grew up to be very good and wise. He did so many good things and said so many wise things that at last his master set him free.

Then he went to live at the court of a great king, who thought Æsop so wise that he gave him more honour than any other wise man at his court. Æsop became famous and rich.

He told stories to princes and kings, and many other great folk. They loved to listen to him, not only because they liked stories, but because each story they heard helped them to be better and greater men.

Whenever Æsop saw people doing a wrong or a cruel thing, he used to tell them a story. In the story he tried to show them how wrong they were. Sometimes they listened and were ashamed. Sometimes they were angry.

Æsop's stories were mostly about animals, and he made the animals talk and act just as men do. Many people then thought that animals were more like us than they really are; so that his stories of animals did not seem at all strange. Stories of this kind are called fables.

When Æsop was an old man, and still telling his wonderful tales, he made some of his listeners very angry. They planned to kill him in order to get rid of him and the stories he told, many of which made them feel ashamed.

They did kill him, but they could not kill his stories. These were all well known and were written down after his death; and now they are told in many, many languages, so that every one may read them.

I wonder if you will like those given in this book. If you do, perhaps your teacher will get some more to read to you, or for you to read.

The Lion and the Mouse

Once upon a time a Lion lay down to rest beneath a big oak tree. He soon fell asleep, but woke with a jump as he felt something running over his back.

It was a little Mouse. Angry at being disturbed, the Lion jumped up, and clapped his great paw on the tiny thing, meaning to kill it.

"Oh, please, please, do let me go!" begged the little Mouse. "I didn't mean to wake you! You are so big and brave and mighty that surely you cannot be so mean as to kill a tiny, harmless thing like me!"

The Lion looked at the little Mouse, and thought for a moment. Then he lifted his paw again, and let him go.

"Very well," he said, "I will set you free. I am not unkind, and you beg so hard for your life."

"Oh, thank you!" cried the Mouse, running off joyfully. "Some day I will repay you for your kindness to me!"

The Lion smiled to hear this, for he thought such a tiny animal could never help *him!*

But some days later, as the Lion was hunting in the forest, he was caught in a net made of rope, which some hunters had put there to trap him. The more he struggled, the more the net closed around him, until at last the Lion could hardly move. He began to roar with anger and pain.

Far away in the forest the little Mouse heard the voice of his friend the Lion.

"Perhaps I can help him!" he cried, and ran off at once.

He came to where the great Lion lay trapped, and saw the net all around him.

"I will set you free!" he cried. "Lie still, my big friend."

The Lion wondered what the little Mouse could do, but he lay still.

Then the Mouse began to nibble and nibble at the rope-net with his sharp little teeth, till— snap! he had bitten one rope through, and— snip! another, and then another, until there was quite a big hole in the net.

"Lie still a little longer!" cried the Mouse, nibbling faster than ever. "Soon I shall have made a way for you to get out!"

And very soon he had bitten through so many ropes that the Lion was able to creep out, and leave the broken net behind him.

"Thank you, my little friend," he cried, as he ran through the forest. "I *am* glad I spared your life the other day!"

Exercises

1. Fill in the blanks:—

Æsop was a ___ boy.

His stories were called ___.

___ talk and ___ in most of the stories.

Æsop made the people listen to stories when
they were ___ ___

2. When was the Lion angry with the Mouse?
3. When was he pleased with him?
4. Pick out all the words in the story which mean
"spoke."

CUTTING SUGAR-CANE

LESSON 23

IN THE SUGAR-CANE FIELDS

WHAT are those children doing over there? They are all very happy sucking their sugar-cane.

It is crop-time now, and men are cutting down the tall stems with their cutlasses. The women are gathering the canes in small bundles, and helping to load the carts and wagons.

See how the mules, horses, oxen, and donkeys are busy pulling away the loaded carts and wagons to the mills!

Some men and women are loading the cane on trucks, to be hauled to the factory by small engines. In Guyana, punts or scows on the punt-trenches or streams are used for this.

There is sunshine everywhere, and gladness beams on the faces of the children. Watch them peeling the dry, brittle skins with their strong, white teeth.

Most of the canes are heavy, and they measure from ten to fourteen feet in length.

Can you tell to what family the sugar-cane belongs? Of course— to the "grass family"; it is really a big grass.

SUGAR CANE
(SECTION AND FLOWER)

The stem is jointed, and it contains a grey pith which is full of sweet, sticky juice. The leaves of the sugar-cane are very like those of the maize or corn.

The plants are mostly grown from "cuttings". If pieces of canes are planted in the soil they will form roots and send up a large number of shoots.

About Christmas-time you may see the flowers. See how beautiful they look in the picture! They

SUGAR-CANE IN FLOWER

are growing on the stems which shoot out from the tops of the plants. They look like plumes or feathers.

Look well at some of the flowers. They are light grey in colour. Touch them. They feel soft and silky. What are those tiny black things like dots, that have fallen from the flowers? They are the seeds, which will grow if carefully sown.

The first crop of canes reaped after the "cuttings" have been planted is called "plant canes." They take from twelve to fourteen months to become ripe. When these are cut, the roots are left in the ground. They are called "stools," and from them new shoots will grow. These new shoots are called "ratoons." Ratoon canes may be reaped up to the end of the fifth year. After this the crop is usually poor, so they are dug up and new canes planted.

Exercises

1. Fill in the blanks:—
      Crop begins in ____ and ends in ____.
      The factories are sometimes called ____.
2. How do we get new plants in the cane-fields?
3. How are the canes taken to the factory?
4. When do the flowers appear?
5. What are ratoons?
6. Which part of the plant is of most use to us?
7. What other plants do you know which belong to the grass family?
8. Draw a sugar-cane flower.

LESSON 24

THE THREE FOOLISH PEOPLE

I

ONCE upon a time there was a farmer who had an only daughter. The girl was very pretty, and a certain young man who lived not far from her father's farm wished to marry her.

Every evening he used to come to see her, and he always stayed to supper with the farmer and his wife. Before they sat down, the daughter would go into the cellar* to fetch a jug of cider.†

One evening she went as usual to draw the cider. As she was doing so, she happened to look up at the ceiling, and she saw a mallet lying across one of the beams. She had not noticed it before, and the sight of it set her thinking.

"Suppose," she said, "that when I am married my husband were to come down

---

* A *cellar* is a cool room under the house.
† *Cider* is a drink made from the juice of apples.

here to draw the cider, and the mallet were to fall on his head and kill him! What a dreadful thing it would be!"

So dreadful did it appear to be that she put down the candle and the jug and sat down to cry.

Soon those upstairs began to wonder how it was that the girl took such a long time to draw the cider; and at last her mother went down to see what she was doing. She found the girl sitting on a wooden seat crying as if her heart would break.

"Why, whatever is the matter?" asked the mother.

"O mother, look at that horrid mallet," said the girl. "Suppose I were to be married, and one day my husband were to come here to draw cider, and the mallet were to fall on his head and kill him, what a dreadful thing it would be!"

"Dear, dear!" said the mother. "It would be dreadful indeed." Then she sat down beside her daughter and started to cry too.

After a while the father came down to see what was the matter with his wife and daughter. They told him why they were crying.

"Dear, dear, dear!" he said. "It would be dreadful, to be sure." Then he sat down beside the other two and began to cry to keep them company.

Before long the young man upstairs began to grow tired of staying in the kitchen by himself. So he too came downstairs, and there he found all three crying side by side, and the cider running from the tap all over the floor.

At once he ran to the cask and turned off the tap. Then he said, "Whatever is the matter with you all?"

"Oh!" said the father, "look at that horrid mallet. Suppose you were to be married, and were to come down here one day to draw the cider, and the mallet were to fall on your head and kill you! Wouldn't that be a dreadful thing?"

Then all three began to cry more loudly than ever; but the young fellow began to laugh.

Reaching up to the beam, he took down the mallet and then said—

"I have travelled many miles, but I have never met three people as foolish as you are. Now I will start on my travels again; and if I can find three people more foolish than you, I will come back to be married. If I can't, I won't!"

So he wished them good-bye at once, and started off on his travels. And the girl cried more than ever because now she had lost her sweetheart.

II

The young man went a long way, and at last came to an old woman's cottage, on the roof of which some grass was growing.

Now the old woman was trying to get her cow to go up a ladder to the grass, but the poor thing was not used to climbing ladders. The young man asked the old woman what she was doing.

"Why, look at all that beautiful grass. I want to get my cow up on the roof to eat it. She will be quite safe, for I will tie a rope round her neck and pass it down the chimney. Then I will tie the other end to my wrist, so that she cannot fall off without my knowing it."

"O you foolish woman!" said the young man. "You ought to cut the grass and throw it down to the cow."

But the old woman thought it was easier to get the cow up the ladder than to get the grass down. So she pushed her and coaxed her till at last she got her up. Then she tied a rope to the cow's neck, passed it down the chimney, and fastened the other end to her own wrist.

The young man went on his way with a merry laugh. But he had not gone far when the cow tumbled off the roof and hung down the side of the house by the rope which was tied round her neck. And the weight of the cow tied to her wrist pulled the old woman up the chimney. If the young man had not cut the rope the cow would have been strangled and the old woman choked with the soot.*

---

* *Soot* is the black dust which lines the chimney. It is formed from the smoke of the fire.

Well, that was *one* person more foolish than the three in the farmer's house.

*   *   *   *   *   *   *   *   *

In a very interesting book, called *A Book of Silly People,* you can read more of the travels of the young man and learn whether he found two others more foolish than those in the cellar. It also contains some more stories of silly people which are very funny.

EXERCISES

1. Fill in the blanks so as to show exactly what the young man really meant when he said, "If I can't ____ I won't ____."
2. Choose the six words from the story which would go best under the picture.
3. Suppose you had gone down into the cellar; say exactly what you would have done.
4. Find these words in the story, and then use them in sentences of your own:—
    to keep them company.
    more than ever.
    the roof of which.
    without my knowing it.
5. Do you think the young man will find two more foolish people? Try to finish the story yourself, making him do so.

LESSON 25

THE THREE LITTLE PIGGIES

A JOLLY old sow once lived in a sty,
  And three little piggies had she,
And she waddled about, saying, "Umph!
      Umph! Umph!"
  While the little ones said, "Wee! Wee!"

"My dear little brothers," said one of the brats,
  "My dear little piggies," said he,
"Let us all for the future say, 'Umph!
      Umph! Umph!'
  'Tis so childish to say, 'Wee! Wee!'"

Then these little pigs grew skinny and lean,
   And lean they might very well be,
For somehow they *couldn't* say, "Umph!
      Umph! Umph!"
   And they *wouldn't* say, "Wee! Wee! Wee!"

So after a time these little pigs died,
   They all died of *felo-de-se*,
From trying too hard to say, "Umph!
      Umph! Umph!"
   When they could only say, "Wee! Wee!"

A moral there is to this little song,
   A moral that's easy to see;
Don't try while young to say, "Umph!
      Umph! Umph!"
   For you can only say, "Wee! Wee!"

Sir Alfred Scott-Gatty
*(By permission of the Author and of
Messrs Metzler & Co. (1920) Ltd)*

Note.—Felo-de-se means killing one's self.

Exercises

1. A moral is a lesson. What lesson can you learn
   from the three little piggies?
2. What sort of a pig was the mother?
3. Do you think she was fat or not? Why?
4. Write these words out in full—"couldn't, wouldn't,
   that's, and 'tis."

LESSON 26

INSECTS—II

In the last lesson on insects you learned how to know one when you see it. Other insects, whose names were not given, are caterpillars, grubs, cotton stainers, maggots, crickets, grasshoppers, cockroaches, hard-backs, and lady-birds.

Caterpillars and grubs do not look much like insects. But after they have eaten a great deal they go to sleep in some quiet nook, and by-and-by they wake up as complete insects such as you read about in the former lesson.

Look at them all and see if they have the right number of legs. The true legs of the caterpillar are at the front of the body.

You also learnt that insects exist in very large numbers. There are so many, and they increase so quickly, that they would cover the earth if there were plenty of food for them and no enemies to check them.

Birds, frogs, and toads destroy many of them or else everything would be eaten up and we should starve. You may have read in the Bible of the plague of locusts.

Some insects are good friends to man, but many are his enemies. Our friends do a great deal of good by killing others which would cause damage. Lady-birds feed upon plant-lice and other small insects. But ants and borers destroy

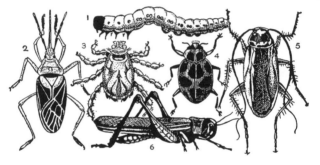

1 CATERPILLAR   2 COTTON STAINER   3 CATTLE TICK
4 LADY-BIRD   5 COCKROACH   6 GRASSHOPPER

crops, while others, such as mosquitoes, suck the blood of man, and ticks do the same to animals.

Some insects supply us with things we need, and these also we can call our friends. Bees give us honey and wax, while silk is made by a small insect, the silkworm.

Insects breathe through little openings in their sides. On many of them a row of tiny spots can be seen on each side where these holes are.

Some insects are seen only at night, and others come out in daylight. They are found in many places. Crickets and grasshoppers can be found on the ground. Butterflies, moths, and bees are near flowers, while others keep to gardens, manure-heaps, ponds, streams, and other damp places.

You will learn more of the life of an insect in the lesson on "Wasps, Butterflies, and Moths," in another book.

Exercises

1. Fill in the blanks:—
   > Hard-backs fly into houses in the ____.
   > There are many ____ in the sides of insects.
   > ____ and ____ are enemies of insects.
   > Moths fly at ____, but butterflies fly during the ____.

2. Write as many names as you can in each of these three lists:—

Insect Enemies of Man	Insect Friends of Man	Useful Insects

LESSON 27

COFFEE

THREE good drinks that most boys and girls like are tea, coffee, and cocoa, or chocolate as you sometimes call it. You know that the tea-plant is not grown in our country, but that both coffee and cocoa are common.

Look at the picture opposite, and you can tell that it is a branch of a coffee tree. You may have seen such a tree growing, and perhaps have one in your garden.

The Blue Mountain coffee of Jamaica is said to be among the best in the world. Much, too, is grown in Guyana, while a little is found in most of the islands.

Perhaps you have dried some berries on a mat near your house, and have roasted them afterwards; so now let us learn something about this very useful tree.

Planters do not allow the tree to grow to its full size, as it would be blown about too much by the wind. They trim it down or "top" it, as it is called, and keep it about five or six feet high. This makes it easier to pick the berries.

Banana plants are used to shade the young trees, but they are cut down when the coffee trees are strong, as these like the full light of the sun then.

The leaves of the coffee plant are evergreen, thick, and shiny. A coffee field is a pretty sight when the trees are in bloom. The flowers are small, and white in colour.

After the flowers fall the berries form in little clusters as you see in the picture. They are red and contain a sweet, yellow pulp. Inside this are two seeds packed snugly together with their flat sides close to each other. You can see these in the picture, where part of the pulp has been cut away.

It is from these seeds or beans that we get the brown powder called coffee, from which the drink is made. The beans are not brown, but green, and they do not smell like coffee. Much has to be done to them before they are ready for the coffee-pot.

The pulp and skin are taken off and the beans are dried in the sun. They are then sent in ships to other countries. In the factory they are first tossed over a fire until they are browned or roasted. This changes the colour and gives them their flavour.

The crisp brown beans are next ground in another machine to give us the brown powder or coffee, which can be bought in packets in the stores or shops. If you live in the country, perhaps you roast and grind the beans for yourselves.

Exercises

Fill in the blanks:—

1. Put in the colour for each of these:—

      The flowers are _____.

      The leaves are _____.

      The berries are _____.

      The pulp is _____.

      The seeds are _____ at first.

      They are _____ after roasting.

2. In six berries there are _____ seeds or beans.

3. When the beans are _____ it gives them their flavour.

4. Planters _____ the tree to keep it short.

5. Coffee trees need _____ shade than cocoa trees.

LESSON 28

GRIMM'S FAIRY TALES

Introduction.—All children love fairy tales, for the fairies love children, and do not make friends so quickly with grown-up people. Now this tale you are going to read is one of the old fairy tales which the brothers Grimm gathered together a hundred years ago. They are really folk-tales, like those you read of in Lesson 8, but were first told in other countries. Children have always loved to hear them. Perhaps if you like this one very much, and your teacher knows you want more, she may give you your wish and get the book with the others in it.

RUMPELSTILTSKIN

I

ONCE upon a time there was a miller who had a very beautiful daughter. Her father was never tired of boasting about her loveliness and all the wonderful things she could do.

It happened one day that the miller had to go to the palace to see the King on business, and as he wanted to appear very grand and important, he said to the King, "Your Majesty has very good straw here in the royal barns, but I have a daughter who can spin straw into gold."

"Indeed," said the King, "she must be very clever. Send her up to the palace at once." For the King was very fond of gold.

The miller began to feel very unhappy, and to wish that he had not boasted quite so much, but it was too late now. So he took his daughter up to the palace, and as soon as the King saw her, he led her into a large room filled with straw. There he gave her a stool and a spinning-wheel, and said, "Now, pretty one, see how quickly you can spin this straw into gold. I will come back to-morrow morning, and if it is not done then, you shall be put to death."

The poor maiden was in great distress. She had never heard of such a thing as spinning straw into gold. She wept and wept till she could scarcely see, and then suddenly she heard a door creak, and a funny little man came hopping into the room.

"What are you crying about?" he asked. "You will spoil your pretty eyes if you do not stop. Tell me what is the matter."

"O sir," sobbed the maiden, "the King has ordered me to spin all this straw into gold before to-morrow morning. If it is not done I shall lose my life, and I don't even know how to begin."

"Now what will you give me if I spin it for you?" asked the little man.

"I will give you my beautiful necklace," she answered gladly.

Then the dwarf sat down at the spinning-wheel and began to spin. Whir, whir, went the straw through his fingers, and out it came in shining threads, till all the straw was gone and the gold thread lay in a glistening heap.

"Good-bye," said the little man, taking the necklace and making a low bow. And before the miller's daughter could say "Thank you," he had hopped out of the room.

II

Next morning the King came very early to see if the straw was really turned into gold. He could scarcely believe his eyes when he saw the shining pile, but it only made him want more. He led the maiden away quickly to another room, bigger than the first and also filled with straw, and told her that she must spin that into gold too.

"If it is not done by to-morrow morning you will know what to expect," he said.

She sat down by the spinning-wheel and began to weep more bitterly than ever, for though she had watched the little dwarf spinning the straw, she did not know at all how it was turned into gold.

But the moment she began to weep, the door flew open and the little man came hopping in just as he had done the day before.

"Come, come," he said, "no more tears! What will you give me if I help you again?"

"I will give you my diamond ring," said the maiden joyfully. And again the dwarf sat down at the spinning-wheel, and the wheel went whizzing round and round till all the straw was spun into threads of gold.

"Oh, thank you, thank you!" cried the maiden. But the dwarf was gone before she could say another word.

III

The King's eyes sparkled with pleasure when he came next morning and saw the large pile of gold.

"This is really a wonderfully clever little maiden," he said to himself.

Then he took her to a still larger room filled with straw, and smiling kindly at her, he said, "If you can spin all this straw into gold before to-morrow morning, I will marry you and you shall be Queen."

The King had scarcely been gone a moment when in hopped the little dwarf again.

"What will you give me this time, if I do your work for you?" asked the manikin.

Now the maiden had nothing more to give, and did not know what to do.

"You can make me a promise," the dwarf said. "When you are Queen, you shall give your first little baby to me."

The maiden thought there was little chance of her ever being Queen, so she promised, caring only about saving her life.

Then the dwarf began spinning again, and worked so merrily that the last handful of straw was soon spun into gold, and the golden pile almost reached the ceiling.

The next morning the King came as usual, and was so delighted that he began to prepare at once for the wedding. He gave her the most beautiful clothes and shining jewels, and they drove away together in a golden coach to church and were married.

IV

The Queen was now so happy that she never once thought of her promise to the little dwarf. And when a beautiful little baby was born, the Queen was happier than ever.

"I shall never know what it is to be sad again," she said.

But at that very moment a door creaked, and, looking up, the Queen saw the same little dwarf come hopping in, just as he had done when he had come to spin the straw into gold.

"What do you want?" asked the Queen holding her baby more tightly, and looking at the dwarf with frightened eyes.

"I want the baby," answered the little man. "Have you forgotten your promise?"

Then the poor Queen remembered how she had said she would give her first little baby to the dwarf, and she burst into tears.

"Oh, take anything else, only leave me my baby!" she cried. And she sobbed so bitterly that the dwarf was quite sorry for her. He wanted the baby very much, but he had a kind little heart, and he thought he would give the Queen one more chance.

"If you can find out what my name is in three days, you shall keep your child," he said. And then he hopped quickly away.

The Queen could not sleep all night, but lay awake thinking of all the names she had ever heard. And when the little man came in the morning she began guessing the longest and most difficult names she could think of.

But to every name the dwarf answered with a merry grin, "No, that is not my name."

The next day the Queen sent messengers over all the country to collect all the curious names they could find, and when the little man appeared she asked, "Is it Spindle-shanks, or Squint-eye, or Bandy-legs?"

"No, it is not!" shouted the little man, hugging himself with joy.

Then the Queen grew terribly anxious, for there was only one day left, and she sent more and more messengers out to search for fresh names.

But the messengers came back to say they could find no new names, and only one had a story to tell. He said he had searched far and near until he came to the wildest part of a dark mountain. There, on the edge of a pine forest, where even the fox and the hare were afraid to go, he had come upon a little man dancing and shouting in front of a tiny red-roofed cottage. There was a fire outside the little house, and the little man had evidently been baking, for he had a tray of freshly baked loaves on his head, and they bounced up and down as he danced and sang,—

"To-day I brew, to-night I bake,
To-morrow I shall the Queen's child take;
For, guess as she may, she never can know
That my name is Rumpelstiltskin, O."

Then the Queen clapped her hands with joy, for she was sure the little man was no other than the dwarf who was coming to take away her baby.

V

Very early next morning the dwarf arrived, and very gaily he hopped into the Queen's room. He was sorry for her grief, but then how nice it was to think of carrying off the baby to live with him in the little red cottage on the edge of the pine wood! He had brought a soft white blanket to roll it in, for he was a kind-hearted little dwarf, and did not want the baby to catch cold.

So he spread out the blanket ready, and then turned to the Queen and said gaily, "Well, have you guessed my name?"

The Queen was smiling too, but she pretended she was still trying to guess.

"Is it William?" she asked.

"No, it is not!" shouted the little man gleefully.

"Is it George?" she said.

"No, it is not!" cried the little man, hopping round on one leg.

"Is it John?" she asked sadly, as if she had come to the end of her questions.

"No, it is not John!" laughed the little man.

"Then it must be Rumpelstiltskin!" cried the Queen.

"The witches must have told you! The witches must have told you! Oh, bother the witches!" screamed the little man, dancing with rage. He stamped his foot so hard that it went right through the floor, and he could not pull it out again. Then he seized it with both hands, and tugged and pulled until the leg was pulled quite off, and he had to hop away on one leg back to his little cottage. And the Queen never saw Rumpelstiltskin again.

Exercises

I

Fill in the blanks:—

1. The King lives in a ____.
2. The miller ____ about his clever ____.
3. She could not ____ straw into ____.
4. Two words in this lesson mean "cried", they are ____ and ____.
5. The maiden took her ____ from her ____ to give to the dwarf.

II

1. What did the King do when he saw the gold?
2. Why was the man called a dwarf?
3. Did the wheel turn fast or slowly?
4. How do you know?

III

Fill in the blanks:—
1. The King wanted to become ＿＿.
2. The first time the dwarf had the maiden's ＿＿, the second time her ＿＿ ＿＿.
3. They rode in a ＿＿ ＿＿ to the ＿＿.
4. The ＿＿ daughter became ＿＿.

IV

1. What did the Queen forget?
2. Why did the messengers go all over the country?
3. How did the Queen know the right name?
4. Where did Rumpelstiltskin live?

V

Fill in the blanks:—
1. The dwarf came to the ＿＿ very ＿＿ for the baby.
2. The blanket was ＿＿ and ＿＿.
3. In this part of the story there are ＿＿ questions.
4. The dwarf was ＿＿ when the Queen ＿＿ his name.

LESSON 29

THE CALENDAR

Note for Teacher.—As an exercise in oral reading this lesson is best read as a dialogue in parts. Select the pupils for the various parts first, and then the words in italics should not be spoken.

After this has been done, an additional exercise might be to change the day of the month and of the week to suit the actual date on which the lesson is being read.

Master. What day of the month is it?

First Pupil. It is the twenty-ninth.

Master. What month is this?

Second Pupil. It is April. To-day is the twenty-ninth of April.

Master. What was yesterday?

Third Pupil. Yesterday was the twenty-eighth of April.

Master. What will to-morrow be?

Fourth Pupil. It will be the thirtieth of April, the last day of the month.

Master. What will the day after to-morrow be?

Fifth Pupil. It will be the first of the next month; that is, the first of May.

Master. What is the day of the week?

Sixth Pupil. To-day is Monday.

Master. What day was it yesterday?

Seventh Pupil. Yesterday was Sunday. The day before yesterday was Saturday.

Master. The days of the week are—Sunday, Monday, Tuesday, Wednesday, Thursday, Friday, and Saturday. Which of these days are holidays?

Eighth Pupil. Saturday and Sunday are holidays.

Master. Here is a nonsense rhyme about the days of the week:—

> "Solomon Grundy,
> Born on a Monday,
> Christened on Tuesday,
> Married on Wednesday,
> Sickened on Thursday,
> Worse on Friday,
> Died on Saturday,
> Buried on Sunday.
> This is the end
> Of Solomon Grundy."

How many months are there in the year?

Ninth Pupil. There are twelve months in the year.

Master. Name them.

Tenth Pupil. January, February, March, April, May, June, July, August, September, October, November, December.

Master. How many days are there in a month?

Eleventh Pupil. There are not the same number in all the months. There are thirty days in some months, and thirty-one in others; and in one month there are only twenty-eight.

Master. You may all say this together:—

"Thirty days have September, April, June, and November:
All the rest have thirty-one, excepting February alone.
Twenty-eight days in February appear,
And one day more is added each leap year."

How often does leap year come?

Twelfth Pupil. Generally every fourth year is leap year.

Master. How many days are there in a year?

Thirteenth Pupil. There are generally three hundred and sixty-five days in a year.

Master. How many days are there in a leap year?

Fourteenth Pupil. There are three hundred and sixty-six days in a leap year.

Master. How many weeks are there in a year?

Fifteenth Pupil. There are fifty-two weeks in a year.

EXERCISES

1. Name the first three days of the week. Name the rest.
2. Name the first, third, and fifth days of the week. Name the rest.
3. Name a month that has thirty days. What other months have the same number?
4. Name a month that has thirty-one. Name the rest that have the same number.
5. On what day did Solomon Grundy die?
6. Which is the first day of the week? Which is the last?
7. Learn how to spell the names of the days and months.
8. One letter comes in all the first four and last four months. What is it?
9. Make up a calendar for the next five weeks, showing the days of the month and week.

LESSON 30

THE FLYING-FISH

ALL West Indian or Guyanese children know that Barbados is often called the "Land of the Flying-Fish," but they may not all know how it earns that name.

Perhaps you have learned that there are some birds which cannot fly. This is not more strange than to be told that there is a wonderful fish which can leave the water and fly for some distance. This fish is called the flying-fish.

It is found in that part of the ocean which washes the West Indian Islands. As the water round Barbados contains many of these fishes, you can see how it gets its name of the "Land of the Flying-Fish."

When this little fish is full-grown it is from eight to nine inches long. Its back is of a dark-blue colour, while the rest of its body is covered with small white scales which shine like silver.

Besides two small fins, it has two larger ones about five inches long. Each of these long fins has ribs which are joined by a thin skin as clear as glass.

When the fish wants to fly, it rises to the surface of the water, spreads out these long fins or wings, as we may call them, and moves through the air until they become dry. Then with a short touch on the waves to wet them again, it flies on once more.

As the fishes skim about near the bows of a ship they look just like birds on the wing, and sometimes they fall on the deck of the vessel.

They live in deep water and swim in large shoals, or schools, as the fishermen call them.

The passing of a bird is enough to scare them and make them sink rapidly, as they are very shy. At other times they surround the boats and seem waiting to be caught.

Then the men throw out their nets and catch the fish as fast as they can. When they have taken as many as their boats can carry they set sail and speed away homewards.

The people in the fishing-villages rejoice as the boats come in sight, and the children run to the beach to greet them.

When there has been a great catch the fishermen blow large shells, and the people for miles around are glad to hear the sound, for it tells the welcome news that flying-fish will be very cheap.

EXERCISES

1. Use your ruler to draw a line eight inches long. On this line draw the body of a fish. Now on each side of the head behind the gills draw a line five inches long. On these lines make the large fins. You have now a good idea of the size of the flying-fish.
2. In what way is this fish like a bird? In what ways is it not like a bird?
3. How are the fishes caught?
4. Why do people like to hear the conch-shell?
5. How many fins has the flying-fish?
6. Why does it rest on the water in its flight?

LESSON 31

ÆSOP'S FABLES—II

Introduction.—Here are some more of Æsop's stories, of which you read in Lesson 22.

THE ASS IN THE LION'S SKIN

ONE day an Ass found the skin of a lion.

"Ah!" he thought, "it would be a good joke to put this skin on, and go and frighten all the sheep and cattle in the fields!"

So he put it over him, and ran to the fields where the sheep were feeding.

"Baa! Baa!" they cried in fright, and ran to crouch by the hedge.

The Ass was pleased. "Now I'll frighten the cows!" he said, and ran into the next field.

Away rushed the cows in terror, thinking a lion had come to eat them.

Suddenly the Ass saw his master coming. "I'll give him a fright too!" he thought.

So he ran up to him; but his master, looking at him closely, saw his long donkey's ears sticking out of the lion's skin, and knew him to be his own Ass and no lion.

The master ran up to him, lifted his stout stick, and began to beat the Ass, so that he brayed in fright.

"There!" said the master; "that will teach you that although you are dressed in a fierce lion's skin, you are really no more than a stupid Ass!"

The Ass went slowly home, feeling very sore and humble.

The Dog and his Bone

A Dog once stole a bone, and ran away with it.
He came to a stream which had a wooden bridge
over it. Just as he got to the middle of the bridge
he looked down, and saw in the clear water
another dog, carrying a bone which he thought
much bigger than his own.

He did not know, of course, that it was his
own reflection in the water. So he snapped at the
dog he saw, hoping to rob him of his big bone.

Splash! Into the water went his own bone as
he opened his mouth to snap.

Slowly it sank down to the bottom of the
stream, and the greedy Dog went on his way
very sadly, wishing he had not lost the real bone
by snapping at the reflection of one!

The Goose with the Golden Eggs

Once upon a time a farmer had a wonderful
Goose. This Goose laid a large golden egg every
single day of her life, and the man knew that one
day he would really be quite rich.

But he was greedy and could not wait.

"If I kill the Goose, I shall be able to have *all*
the golden eggs inside her that she is going to lay

in the future!" he thought. "It is a good idea, for if I can get them all at once, I shall be a rich man without having to wait from day to day!"

So he took a knife and killed the Goose. But when he looked inside its body, do you think the foolish man found golden eggs? No, of course he didn't!

"Oh dear me!" he cried sadly; "I have killed my goose that laid the golden eggs! I wish I had been wise enough to wait for her to lay them day by day."

But it was much too late then for such a wish!

The Dog in the Manger

ONCE there was a Dog who was very sleepy. He looked about for a nice soft bed to lie down in.

"I know there is hay in the cowshed," he thought. "I'll go there and lie on it."

So he trotted into the cowshed and jumped into a manger full of soft, sweet hay. Then he lay down and went to sleep.

Presently a Cow came up to the manger to eat her meal of hay. In trying to pull out some hay she woke the Dog, and he sprang up fiercely. "Go away!" he snapped. "Can't you see I'm here? I won't have you touching this hay!"

"You don't want it yourself," said the Cow. "You don't eat hay!"

"What does that matter!" barked the Dog. "I'm not going to let *you* eat it either," and the selfish little creature curled himself up once more in the manger.

The Cow turned to the others. "What a selfish Dog!" she said. "He can't eat the hay himself, and yet he won't let others have it!"

And all of them stared at the Dog in disgust.

Exercises

1. Which of these five fables do you like best? Why?
2. Which animal showed kindness?
3. Make up a little story like "The Dog in the Manger" about a boy and a very large box of candies.
4. Is there any way of turning eggs into money?
5. One of the animals was *selfish,* one was *stupid,* one was *greedy,* and one was *grateful.* Name each of them.
6. Try to draw a little picture to go with the story "The Dog and his Bone."

READING TESTS AND EXERCISES

(These are given as suggestions for the teacher. Others of a similar nature can be devised to cultivate the individual power of reading on the part of the pupils.)

TEST I

Write out the names of all the *trees* given in this book, with the numbers of the pages on which they are found, thus,—

> Mango tree, pages 9, 10, 25, etc.
> Lime tree, page 10, etc.
> Coconut tree, page 50, etc.

TEST II

Do the same with the *animals* mentioned.

TEST III

Names of places are always spelt with capital letters. Write out all the names of places given in this book, with the numbers of the pages, as in Test I.

TEST IV

On what pages do you find these words:—

> Chest, fierce, feathers, cities, kernel, snake, surprise, flavour, skinny, gardens, sunshine, proverb?

TEST V

On page 41 you are told of two animals who were very friendly. The words are, "The dog and the agouti were close friends."

Write out the words which tell you each of these things, and give the number of the page on which the words are found:—

(*a*) He thought it over many times.
(*b*) An animal laughed.
(*c*) I have been on many journeys.
(*d*) One part of a plant is like a little box.
(*e*) An animal walked about slowly.
(*f*) I left my home.
(*g*) Wood is used in making ships.
(*h*) To be polite is better than to be rude.

TEST VI

THE PRINCESS AND THE FROG

(*Try to make out this story from the words and phrases here given. The picture on the next page will help you with the first part.*)

I

KING: beautiful daughters: youngest the prettiest.

Castle: forest: deep well.

Youngest Princess: golden ball: play.

Ball in well: tears: more tears.

Tiny voice: Frog on leaf in well.

"What will you give me?"

"Crown: pearls: jewels: anything."

THE PRINCESS AND THE FROG (*W. R. Symonds*).

"No use: love: sit at table: eat from plate: drink from cup: sleep at foot of bed."

"Anything."

Frog dives: ball on edge of well.

Princess runs away with ball: Frog left very sad.

2

King and Princess: dinner: lords and ladies.

Marble staircase: something creeping: splish, splash.

"Little Princess, open to me!"

Opens door: Frog enters: door shut.

"Giant at door?"

"Only nasty frog: playing near well: lost ball: promised to be play-fellow: silly."

"YOU MUST KEEP YOUR PROMISE."

Gentle knock: door opened: Frog enters.

"Place me on table."

"Let me eat and drink with you."

Princess sulky: Frog happy.

"Lay me at foot of golden bed."

3

Princess weeps: "YOU MUST KEEP YOUR PROMISE."

Frog carried upstairs.

Bedroom: Frog dropped on floor.

Changed at once: handsome prince.

Prince's story: changed by witch: only set free by a princess.

Princess sorry: weeps.

Prince very kind: "Marry me."

Coach and eight white horses: footmen at back.

Wedding: happy ever after.

Note to Teacher.—You will find this story in full in *Stories from Grimm*: see "Prefatory Note for Teachers," page iv.

TEST VII

THE TAR BABY

(*You will not find it hard to fill in the gaps in this story if you think a little and look at the picture on page* ii.)

BRER FOX was very hungry. So he made up his mind to catch Brer Rabbit and eat him all up.

He got a lot of tar and made a ___ ___. Then he took this ___ ___ and set it ___ in the ___ of the road by which he knew ___ ___ would come.

Soon Brer Rabbit came down the road, sure enough. And Brer Fox lay behind the bushes and said nothing.

"Good-morning," said Brer Rabbit to the Tar Baby. "A nice, fine morning this is."

But the ___ ___ said ___ at all.

"Are you deaf?" said Brer Rabbit. "Because if you are, I can shout louder."

But ___ ___ ___ ___ nothing at all.

"You are proud, that's what you are," said ___ ___; "and I'm going to cure you."

But ___ ___ ___ ___ ___ ___ all.

"If you don't take off your hat to me," said Brer Rabbit, "I'm going to teach you manners."

Then he drew back his paw and struck the Tar Baby on the head. But his paw stuck fast ___ ___ ___, and he could not get it loose.

And ___ ___ ___ ___ ___ ___ ___.

Next Brer Rabbit struck him with his left fore-paw. This also stuck fast in the tar, and he could not get it loose.

After this Brer Rabbit struck him with each of his hind-paws in turn; and they ___ ___ like the others.

But ___ ___ ___ ___ ___ ___ ___.

Last of all Brer Rabbit struck him with his head, but this also ___ ___ ___ ___ ___. Then Brer Fox came walking up.

"You seem rather stuck up this morning, Brer Rabbit," said he. "I think you will join me at dinner this time."

The Briar Patch

Then Brer Rabbit said to ___ ___, "I don't greatly care what you do with me."

"Not at all?" asked Brer Fox.

"Well," said ___ ___, "you can boil me or roast me if you like, but there is one thing I hope you will not do to me."

"And what is that?" asked Brer Fox, with a sly look in his ___.

"Don't throw me into that briar patch," he said.

"It is too much work to light a fire," said Brer Fox, "so I think I will hang you."

"Hang me as high as you like," said Brer Rabbit, "but do not ___ ___ ___ ___ ___ patch."

"I have no string," said Brer Fox, "so I think I must drown you."

"Drown me as deep as you please," said Brer Rabbit, "but ___ ___ ___ ___ ___ ___ ___ ___."

"There is no water near this place," said Brer Fox, "so I think I must skin you."

"Skin me at once," said Brer Rabbit, "___ ___ ___ ___ ___ ___ ___ ___ ___."

Then Brer Fox said to himself, "It seems I shall hurt him most if I throw ___ ___ ___ ___ ___."

So he did so without waiting any longer.

Brer Rabbit fell into the briar patch, and Brer Fox waited to see what would happen.

By-and-by he heard someone call him. He looked back, and this is what he saw.

He saw Brer Rabbit sitting on a log, taking the tar out of his fur with a chip of wood.

And this is what he heard:—

"I was bred and born in a briar patch; bred and ___ in a ___ patch. Ha! ha! he!"

EXERCISES

1. Where did Brer Fox get the hair for the Tar Baby?
2. Try to draw the Tar Baby, but show its face.

3. If you could paint a picture for the second story,
   what would you show in it?
4. Which was wiser, Brer Fox or Brer Rabbit?

TEST VIII

How the Broad Bean got its Black Seam

THERE was once an old woman who bought a dish of beans for her dinner. She put them into a pot, over a coal fire, to boil.

One of the beans fell out of the pot and lay on the floor near a straw.

Soon afterwards a live coal jumped out of the fire, and fell near the bean and the straw.

"How did *you* get here?" said the coal to the bean.

"Oh," said the bean, "I just slipped away from the old woman, who is boiling my brothers and sisters until their skins burst."

The coal said, "I too got away from her. She is now burning *my* brothers and sisters to cinders."

"What shall we do now?" asked the straw.

"Let us get away from here as soon as we can," said the coal.

The three friends at once set out together. The old woman ran after them, but she could not catch them.

Soon they came to a stream of water.

"What shall we do now?" said they.

The straw said, "I will lay myself across the stream, and you can walk over me."

The coal said it would do so; but the bean wished to stay on *this* side of the stream.

So the straw stretched itself from one bank to the other, and the coal began to cross over.

When it was half-way across the coal grew afraid. It stood still, not daring to go on.

The straw began to burn, and broke in two, and the coal fell with a hiss-s-s into the stream

The bean was safe on shore, and it laughed until it split its coat. And now it thought that it was no better off than its two friends.

A tailor, who was out for a walk, sat down near the stream to rest. He took out his needle and thread, and sewed up the bean's coat.

The bean thought that the tailor was very kind. But the man had used black thread; and now the bean has a black seam, as you can plainly see.

EXERCISES

1. Hold the picture up to the light, so that you can see it through the paper, and try to draw it with the bean running to the left.
2. Draw a dish of beans.
3. Draw an open bean-pod showing five beans.
4. Draw the pot on the fire. (Not a *pan*.)
5. What is a dead coal? Who killed it?
6. What would the straw become when it was burnt?
7. Try to write a verse about the first part of the story. Let me help you:—

   There was an old woman as I've heard tell,
   Who bought some beans and boiled them well.

   —Now go on.
8. Why do you think the bean did not wish to cross the stream?
9. Can you make up a story about how the coconut got its eyes? Or how it lost its brown jacket? If you can, try to put your story into verses.

ADDITIONAL POETRY FOR READING AND RECITATION

If!

IF all the seas were one sea,
What a *great* sea that would be!
And if all the trees were one tree,
What a *great* tree that would be!
And if all the axes were one axe,
What a *great* axe that would be!
And if all the men were one man,
What a *great* man he would be!
And if the *great* man took the *great* axe,
And cut down the *great* tree,
And let it fall into the *great* sea,
What a splish splash *that* would be!

The Little Seed

IN the heart of the seed buried deep, so deep,
A dear little plant lay fast asleep.
"Wake," said the sunshine, "and creep to
    the light."
"Wake," said the voice of the raindrops bright.
The little plant heard it, and rose to see
What the wonderful outside world might be.

THE VOWELS

WE are very little creatures,
All of different voice and features;
One of us in *glass* is set,
One of us you'll find in *jet*.
T'other* you may see in *tin*,
And the fourth a *box* within.
If the fifth you should pursue,
It can never fly from *you*.

                    JONATHAN SWIFT

LITTLE BIRDIE

WHAT does little birdie say
In her nest at peep of day?
Let me fly, says little birdie,
    Mother, let me fly away.
Birdie, rest a little longer,
Till the little wings are stronger.
So she rests a little longer,
    Then she flies away.

What does little baby say,
In her bed at peep of day?
Baby says, like little birdie,
    Let me rise and fly away.

* *T'other* = the other

Baby, sleep a little longer,
Till the little limbs are stronger.
If she sleeps a little longer,
    Baby too shall fly away.

LORD TENNYSON

THE WIND

I SAW you toss the kites on high,
And blow the birds about the sky;
And all around I heard you pass,
Like ladies' skirts across the grass—
    O wind, a-blowing all day long,
    O wind, that sings so loud a song!

I saw the different things you did,
But always you yourself you hid,
I felt you push, I heard you call,
I could not see yourself at all—
    O wind, a-blowing all day long,
    O wind, that sings so loud a song!

O you that are so strong and cold,
O blower, are you young or old?
Are you a beast of field and tree,
Or just a stronger child than me?
    O wind, a-blowing all day long,
    O wind, that sings so loud a song!

From "A Child's Garden of Verses," by
ROBERT LOUIS STEVENSON

I Would Like You for a Comrade

I would like you for a comrade, for I love you,
    that I do,
I never met a little girl as amiable as you;
I would teach you how to dance and sing and
    how to talk and laugh,
If I were not a little girl and you were not
    a calf.

I would like you for a comrade, you should share
    my barley meal,
And butt me with your little horns just hard
    enough to feel;
We would lie beneath the chestnut-trees and
    watch the leaves uncurl,
If I were not a clumsy calf and you a little girl.

From "Katawampus," by
Judge Parry
(By permission of the Author)

How Doth the Little Busy Bee

How doth the little busy bee
    Improve each shining hour,
And gather honey all the day
    From every opening flow'r!

How skilfully she builds her cell!
    How neat she spreads the wax!
And labours hard to store it well
    With the sweet food she makes.

In works of labour or of skill,
    I would be busy too;
For Satan finds some mischief still
    For idle hands to do.

In books, or work, or healthful play,
    Let my first years be passed,
That I may give for ev'ry day
    Some good account at last.

ISAAC WATTS

THE SUNBEAMS

"WHAT shall I send to the earth to-day?"
    Said the great, round, golden sun,
"Let us go down to work and play!"
    Said the sunbeams, every one.

Down to the earth the sunbeams crept,
    To children in their beds,
Touching the eyes of those who slept,
    And gilding the little heads.

"Wake, little children!" they cried in glee,
  "And from dreamland come away!
We've brought you a present! Wake and see!
  We've brought you a sunny day!"

EMILIE POULSSON

MY SHADOW

I HAVE a little shadow that goes in and out with
  me,
And what can be the use of him is more than I
  can see;
He is very, very like me from the heels up to the
  head;
And I see him jump before me, when I jump into
  my bed.

The funniest thing about him is the way he likes
  to grow—
Not at all like proper children, which is always
  very slow;
For he sometimes shoots up taller, like an india-
  rubber ball,
And he sometimes gets so little that there's none
  of him at all.

He hasn't got a notion of how children ought to
    play,
And can only make a fool of me in every sort of
    way.
He stays so close beside me, he's a coward you
    can see;
I'd think shame to stick to nursie as that shadow
    sticks to me!

One morning, very early, before the sun was up,
I rose and found the shining dew on every
    buttercup;
But my lazy little shadow, like an arrant sleepy-
    head,
Had stayed at home behind me and was fast
    asleep in bed!

From "A Child's Garden of Verses," by
ROBERT LOUIS STEVENSON

THE LITTLE FISH THAT WOULD NOT DO AS IT WAS BID

"DEAR mother," said a little fish,
    "Pray is not that a fly?
I'm very hungry, and I wish
    You'd let me go and try."

"Sweet Innocent," the mother cried,
     And started from her nook,
"That horrid fly is put to hide
     The sharpness of the hook."

Now, as I've heard, this little trout
     Was young and foolish too,
And so he thought he'd venture out,
     To see if it were true.

And round about the hook he played,
     With many a longing look,
And— "Dear me," to himself he said,
     "I'm sure that's not a hook.

"I can but give one little pluck:
     Let's see, and so I will."
So on he went, and lo! it stuck
     Quite through his little gill.

And as he faint and fainter grew,
     With hollow voice he cried,
"Dear mother, had I minded you,
     I need not now have died."

                          JANE AND ANN TAYLOR